Creating Family Legacy Movies

Treasure Your Memories

Judy Blair

ISBN: 1511631546

ISBN-13: 978-1511631549

DEDICATION

*To my grandmother, Florence, who is the inspiration for
what I do.*

*I want to thank my husband, Rick, for his support and
understanding for all the hours I spend working at the
computer making movies.*

To get your free Video Preparation Checklist, go to www.keepsakepix.com/free.

To get a free consultation about your family legacy movie, go to www.keepsakepix.com.

Table of Contents

Chapter 1

Introduction

If there is a special person in your life who you treasure and you want to make sure their life, their stories, and their memories are preserved for you, their grandchildren, and future generations, then this book is for you.

It has become my mission in life to help people like you preserve and share their memories.

Why, you ask? Well, let me share a short story with you.

When I was a child growing up in California, my grandmother lived thousands of miles away. Every birthday and Christmas, she'd call me, my sister, and my brother. She would also call in between the holidays. I remember every birthday and Christmas, she would send us each $2. Back in those days, that wasn't bad money for a kid. Years later I noticed the amount had never increased with inflation. But I looked forward to her greeting card with that $2 in it.

When we would talk on the phone she would always called me "darling." She always sounded very loving and affectionate, much more affectionate than my parents. It wasn't that my parents didn't love us, it's just that my mother grew up in a family that didn't show much affection. So I loved talking to my grandmother and loved whenever I got to see her in person.

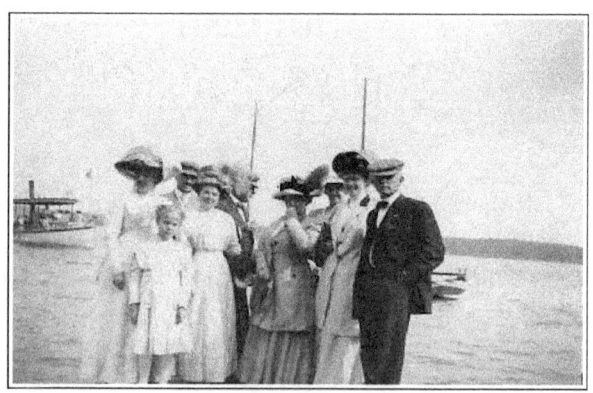

My grandfather died when I was in seventh grade. I remember being at a classmate's home after school when I found out. My memories of him are vague and I can't remember any person-to-person conversations with him. I do know that we spent time together only by the photographs of him and me and my siblings together when we were very young. I know how much my grandmother loved him and that they were very close for all their years together. I have photos of them together in college where they were in stage plays, and of them on dates with groups of friends, some with very old automobiles, and some at the lake. My grandmother was a widow for a very long time and she always talked about him until her death.

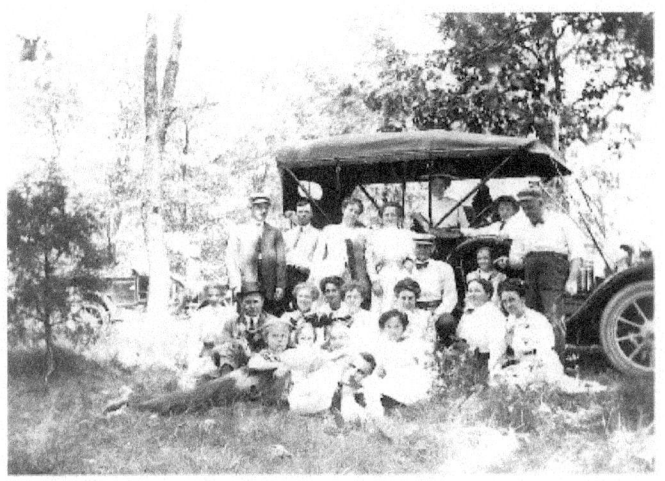

After I graduated from high school, I first went away to college on the west coast for two years. Then I left and went back to live with my grandmother in the Midwest in her small apartment. She had a nice living room/dining room, a smallish kitchen, and one bedroom with two twin beds, one for each of us.

Just before the school year began, I found a job at the university, taking the bus to and from work every day. After a while, I could tell it was getting harder for my grandmother to share her space, as she was used to living alone. She was about 70 years old at the time, and I was still just a teenager.

So, I found a boarding house halfway between her apartment and the university. I rented a room from a woman with two daughters, one at college also, and the other still in high school. I moved there and would walk to Grandma's apartment and spend the weekends with her. Some of my most cherished memories are the ones of talking with my grandmother, hearing about Grandpa, their lives together, and about Dad his little sister. My grandmother and I often had long energizing conversations debating politics.

She had a few very close friends that she introduced me to, and sometimes we would take little excursions. My grandmother didn't drive, so her friends would drive us around to their favorite eating places and tourist attractions. She talked a lot about Grandpa, but over the years I've forgotten many of the details she told me.

I eventually transferred to the University of Wisconsin in Madison and got my degree there. I remember my father flying out to my graduation, even though my family always had to stretch the money they made. My father and my grandmother attended the ceremony. It was one of my proudest moments. They were both very proud also, especially because I was the first of my generation to graduate from college. I'm so thankful that I saved my pictures from that graduation.

How ironic that when my grandmother got older, Dad moved her out to California and the warm weather. I had already moved farther east to Washington D.C., so once again we were separated by miles and we maintained a largely telephone relationship. Years later, when she passed away I felt like a big chunk of unconditional love was gone from my life.

Today, her stories, her history, and her memories are

becoming fainter and fainter. I'm slowly forgetting even what her voice sounded like.

My goal is for you to not have to go through that same thing I went through with my grandmother. And I still lament the fact that I can't see or hear her or my parents. Our parents and grandparents are amazing people who have been there for us as we grew up, teaching us, guiding us, and caring for us. I wish I had recorded time with my grandmother, because I struggle to recall what it sounded like when she said my name. She had so many fun things about her and little quirky traits that I adored, and now, they are all but gone.

In this book, I want to help guide you to preserving and sharing your memories - memories of your parents, your grandparents, and your family. Family is the most important thing we have in this life, and it's vital we preserve the lives of the older generations for the younger generations.

Judy Blair

Chapter 2

Why It Matters

Let's talk about legacy. A family legacy means different things to different people. Typically the definition is "something received from an ancestor or predecessor," like a financial inheritance or some object such as a piece of jewelry. In this book we're going to talk about a different kind of legacy – a personal family legacy, which is keeping your memories, your values, and stories alive for future generations.

There was a recent survey done that said 86% of baby boomers and 74% of Americans age 72 and older believe that documenting family history is the most important legacy that can be passed onto their heirs.

These statistics tell us that the older we get, the more

important our family legacy becomes. It seems that the desire to document our lives and tell our stories runs deep.

Chapter 3

Memories At Risk

Does a shoe box filled with family photos sound familiar to you?

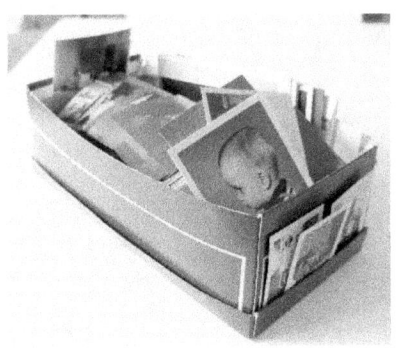

Then perhaps a cardboard box filled with photo albums of various sizes and stages of condition is also something you are familiar with. If these are stored in a garage, basement, or attic and are subject to extreme temperatures and humidity, they are on a slow roller coaster to destruction.

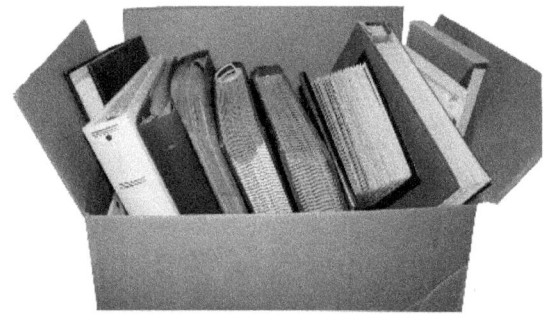

Some of the albums might have magnetic photo pages. When you pick them up, almost all the photos fall out. I still have some of these magnetic albums. Unfortunately, back when I mounted my photos in these types of albums, nobody told me it was a terrible idea. The magnetic pages are hazardous to the health of your photos. The cardboard pages contain acid and lignin which will destroy your photos over time. The plastic pages and sticky glue just add to the ultimate destruction of your valuable photos.

If you store your photos in photo frames and they are subjected to daily light, some of them may be terribly faded, turning colors or otherwise damaged. Some pictures you might not even be able to see very well. You can have them scanned and restored to like-new quality. When you get those photos printed out, if you want to replace the damaged photo in the photo frame, make sure you store a second copy in albums or boxes that are acid, lignin, and PVC free or keep the digital copy in a safe place.

Are you lucky enough to have a treasure of really old dusty family albums?

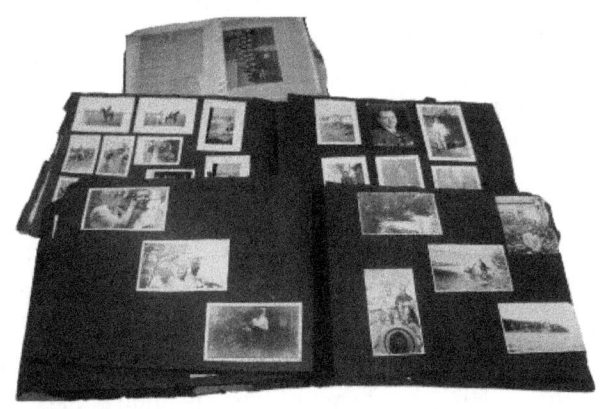

Most of them have black pages. Some have a lot of torn pages, photos that were either glued in or stuck in with photo corners. Some people just glue in the photos, and over time they fall out. Sometimes people scribble a few words on the album page to describe what the pictures are. I personally have some of my mother's albums that were on black photo paper. It's more like just colored paper back in those days. (Those papers weren't acid-free.) She had written in white on those pages describing what the pictures were about and the dates.

Many people treat photos that hold their family legacy as "just a box" that "kinda" gets in the way when you need something in the garage, or something they just leave lying around in a cold attic.

Rest assured that anything film or paper-based will deteriorate over time. A proper storage environment is the best defense against deterioration.

Where and how you store your photos determines how they are directly affected by environment. The main factors affecting their preservation are relative humidity, temperature, air pollution, and light. High, low, and fluctuating relative humidity can cause image deterioration and shrinking and cracking of the binder, thus causing curling of the paper.

High temperature causes a fast rate of deterioration. Combined with high humidity and damaging effects of air pollution, many color dyes will fade and discolor. Paper will also yellow and become brittle, especially if the paper is acidic. High temperature and humidity may also contribute to the growth of microscopic mold spores on the image. Once active mold infests a photograph, it is usually impossible to remove without damaging the photograph.

Most photographic materials are also vulnerable to deterioration caused by light—both sunlight and standard fluorescent light. They are both strong sources of ultraviolet light.

You might be surprised to learn that photos stored on the floor of a garage or basement are vulnerable to damage by water leaks or insects and rodents. Insects (silverfish, beetles, cockroaches) and rodents (rats, mice, and squirrels) are all attracted to photographic materials. If you have photos stored in boxes or cabinets they should be dusted or vacuumed on a regular basis. And, by all means, keep them off the floor!

Tip: If you have older photos that you treasure and want to display, have a copy made of the original and display the copy. Store the original in a safe place – away from light and humidity and off the floor. Be sure to store it in an acid-free, lignin-free envelope or album.

There are a lot of emotions that come up when you mention disorganized photos to someone. For some people they imagine their shoe boxes of old photos in their attic or out on their garage floor and thinking of organizing those may cause panic, overwhelm and dread. Who has time to tackle that monster? And to others, knowing those antique family photos are degenerating more each day causes terrible anguish and feelings of guilt.

Today with the preponderance of smart phones, camcorders, and digital cameras most people take digital photos. Where are your digital photos stored? I know people who have camcorders that are 20 years old and they've got movies and photos on them that they can't access because the camera no longer works or they don't know how to get them off the camcorder into any kind of a usable format. If you don't know how, find someone who can help you, because you may have a wealth of family history on that camera. You'd be surprised at the number of people that have smartphones full of photos, and again, people don't know how to get them from their smartphone to a computer or any kind of a format that they can really use.

Have you ever thought what would happen if your photos are on your phone, and the phone falls out of your pocket or it breaks or falls into water? So what do you do?

Chapter 4

How To Preserve Your Memories

The first big tip is get your photos out of those devices. Get help if necessary if you don't know how to retrieve them. If you lose a camera or your smartphone, all your photos are gone. If it should break and you have to start over with a new phone, all the photos and videos are gone. If you can't find someone with a camcorder that matches yours or if you don't have them converted by a professional service, all those videos are gone. That's the first step: save them. Get them onto your computer.

The second big tip is − back them up! Let's say you've been really good about getting all of your photos onto your computer, and there they sit. The next big question is: Do you have them backed up and where do you back them up? There are a number of options.

- A lot of people use thumb drives. Those are the small flash drives or USB drives that you stick into your computer so you can copy files back and forth. You can store photos on them.

- There are external portable drives that are independent hard drives that connect to your computer with a USB cable into a USB port. You can copy your photos from your computer onto that for storage.

- You can copy them onto CDs.

- There is also cloud storage. What is that? It is a generic term for large computers that store your files. You pay a company a certain amount per month or per year for a designated amount of storage space where you can store files and photos. Dropbox is a really popular one that you may have heard of. Other places like Shutterfly and Mixbook also allow you to upload your photos so you can turn them into photo products. (Just make sure the site allows you to download your photos in their original size if you later need them on your computer.) If you're an Apple product user there's iCloud. There are many other places where you can save your photos online.

- I would actually recommend three layers of photo storage for safekeeping. The first would be your computer. The second would be a USB drive (or thumb drive), CDs, or an external hard drive such as My Passport. Then the third would be cloud storage. In this way you have several layers of backup if anything should happen. Sure, if you have your USB drives, your CDs, and your external hard drives in your house, heaven forbid that your house should catch on fire and they burn up. Then where are you? By having them on a cloud server that protects you further.

I have digital copies of my photos and I've got them backed up. Now what do I do? Some people will organize their photos and put them all on CD. I heard someone who has three children say she put all of the photos of one child on one CD and photos of another child on another CD and gave them to the kids and said she was finished. She thought she'd done her duty. What do those photos really mean to the children? Furthermore, if you've got older family photos with no story around them and you don't know who the people are, what do those photos mean? Have you ever heard someone say "I have boxes of old photos – and I don't know who the people are!"?

I inherited a lot of old family photos. Some are black and white, some are yellowed or discolored with age, and some are sepia-colored. What a treasure! But, for the most part the people in them are all strangers to me. The sad part is I know they are mostly ancestors of mine. But, who are they?

I ran across a poem some time ago that talks about this. It is written by Pam Harazim.

"STRANGERS IN THE BOX"

Come, look with me inside this drawer,
In this box I've often seen,
At the pictures, black and white,
Faces proud, still, serene.
I wish I knew the people,
These strangers in the box,
Their names and all their memories
Are lost among my socks.
I wonder what their lives were like,
How did they spend their days?
What about their special times?
I'll never know their ways.
If only someone had taken time
To tell who, what, where, or when,
These faces of my heritage
Would come to life again.
Could this become the fate
Of the pictures we take today?
The faces and the memories
Someday to be passed away?
Make time to save your stories,
Seize the opportunity when it knocks,
Or someday you and yours could be
The strangers in the box.

Thankfully someone had written on the backs of a lot of my photos so I could piece my family history together with quite a few documents and newspaper articles. If you're lucky you should be able to do that as well.

They say "a picture is worth a thousand words." And it is if you know the people or the story behind the picture. But if you know neither the people nor the story, a picture tells you very little.

If this sounds familiar to you, pull out those photos now! Don't keep putting it off. Talk to family members while they are still around and ask them to help identify them.

But, please don't write names and information in INK on the back of the photo! And even worse, on the front of the photo!! On many of the ones I inherited I had to retouch the photos where the ink bled through the photo. Instead, if you must write on the back, use a pencil and write lightly. Or, write on a sticky note and put it on the back on the margin of the photo. (Have sticky notes been around long enough for us to know what that sticky stuff might do to the photo paper over time?) And don't tape any notes to the photo. We know what sticky tape will do. (I've tried to carefully peel off old tape from a photo before scanning it and it leaves awful marks. What a photo-retouching job that was!) The best thing to do is buy acid-free photo envelopes and write on the envelopes. And, finally, place the photos in the proper acid-free storage medium in a dark, dry, cool place.

Now, how do I organize my photos? You can organize them in various ways.

Some people want to make a serious project of organizing their disorganized photos. It is not the purpose of this book to go into detail about how to do that. There is a very good source if you want to take this on. It is a website called www.organizedphotos.com

They'll help you overcome stumbling blocks, offer an organizing method, suggest what archival quality supplies to purchase, and how to keep your photos and negatives safe.

If you want to organize digital photos, it's easier to do as you upload your photos from your camera(s). Some people organize their photos all by year. I personally organize mine by year, by month, and by event. Some people prefer to organize all their photos according to children's events as they were growing up or events in the past. How ever you choose to organize them, it makes it much more manageable so you can actually do something with those photos.

What do I mean by "do something with your photos"?

When I say "do something," the next step to take is to use them in some kind of a project. The kinds of projects are innumerable. You can make scrapbooks where you write stories around the pictures in scrapbooks. You can use various embellishments, pretty colors, and special paper. There are many services that help you create photo books online. You can document baby's birth, baby's first year, a year in review of your family's activities, Valentine's Day, your trip to Hawaii, your daughter's wedding, your favorite family recipes — the ideas are too many to mention. Again, to make the photo stories memorable, I believe it is critical to supplement the photos with descriptions and stories that tell why the photos are important.

While I do love photos and photo books, and I believe photos are critical to your family's history, they have a big drawback. Photos are of a single moment captured in time. They don't record action. They don't record laughter. They don't record the words and emotions spoken in that moment. And, they don't tell the whole story.

Judy Blair

Chapter 5

The Family Legacy Movie

The family legacy movie is the ultimate way of passing on the stories and lives of older generations to future generations. You can tell a story about where the grandparents were born and where they grew up. You can share wonderful memories, such as weddings and birthdays of your parents. Family legacy movies can give the viewer a sense that they really do know the people they are seeing. Family legacy movies bring the photos to life. You can record laughter, voices, and exciting moments. Best of all, the family legacy movie lets you tell a more complete story of someone's life.

A family legacy movie is more than just a collection of random video snippets. A family legacy movie gives a viewer the feeling that they are really connecting with the subject of the video. They are learning about their family history, discovering and remembering the stories of their loved ones.

I regret not thinking of making a legacy video of my grandmother. While video cameras were not plentiful, they did exist. Audio recorders existed also. Now I have the pain of not being able to relive some of our favorite moments together. Other than a few pictures, I don't remember in detail what her apartment looked like or what she liked to wear. I know what it's like to not have my grandmother's life on video, and I wish I had it.

Even though your grandmother may be gone, you can still make a family legacy movie about her. I've done it for my grandmother, but I've had to use what I have – and that is photos. You, too, can do this by making a video using the photos you have of your grandmother (or other loved one) and putting them into a video editing software program where you can bring the photos to life by making them move on screen. Using a voice recorder (or your computer's recording capability), talk about each photo. Talk about when and where it was taken and the story around it. Then, when you insert the audio into the movie program, you can adjust the length of time for each photo according to the length of the audio. Add your loved one's favorite music for the introduction and ending

It's important to get started on your family legacy movie of your loved ones now before it's too late. In the coming chapters, I'll explain what you can do to get started on your first family legacy movie of a parent, grandparent, or other special family member.

Chapter 6

How To Prepare For The Video

So how do you get started?

First, you'll need to decide that this is something you want to do. You won't get a family legacy movie made if you don't first determine that you want to preserve the memories of your parents, grandparents, or other family members on video. Many people have told me this is something they've thought about for years but they never actually made the decision to do it. This is definitely the most important step. If you don't decide you want to do it, you won't ever get one done. So take the first step — make the decision to do it.

Second, you'll want to decide what the focus of the

video is. Some people might call this the theme of the video. Are you focusing the video on one particular person? Often, family legacy movies are focused on a specific person. Are you focusing on an entire family history? Are you going to focus the video on the major milestones of a person's life? Do you want to try to capture the day-to-day life of the subject? What do you want to do with the video? I find that many of my clients know they want to do a video, normally about a specific person, but don't really know what to focus on or what to include in the video, so I normally help them come up with ideas and pick the best option.

Third, you want to set a date. Don't put it off. You can do one this Saturday, for example. If your video is about a family member you don't see often, set something up around a holiday when you'll be visiting them or they will be visiting you.

Fourth, you want to pick a location. I recommend recording indoors in a quiet room because it's easier to manage with less noise. If you choose an outdoors location the wind can be unpredictable and hard to deal with, as can be the noise of cars or trucks driving by, or construction beginning in the neighborhood on the day you decide to record. If you do want to do it outside, first use a microphone on your subject. Next try to pick a spot that is lightly shaded, or do it on a cloudy but bright day. I don't recommend doing it in the bright sunlight because the subject of the video will be squinting or wearing sunglasses which obscures the face. If your subject likes nature, perhaps record at a city park or a national park. If the subject of the video grew up in a family house that someone in the family still owns, record in the front or back yard of the family house.

Fifth, you want to consider if you want to do it all by yourself, or if you want to get help. In a coming chapter, I'll talk to you about how, why, and where to get help with your video. This is the legacy of a loved one you're putting together, and you want to be sure it's done correctly and well.

If you decide you want to do it by yourself, you'll need to prepare to record. These days, smartphones are capable of recording decent quality video. A 16GB smartphone can hold roughly an hour of HD video. If you use a digital camera to record, an hour of HD video can come in at just under 5GB.

I do have a Video Preparation Checklist I make available to my clients, but I'd also like to give you a free copy of it. You can get it by going to my website at www.KeepsakePix.com/free-pdf.

Judy Blair

Chapter 7

All About Photos

This is one of the most important parts of making a family legacy movie.

The next step is to get your photos together. A lot of people tell me, "I want to do a family legacy video, but first I need to get my photos organized." My answer to that is, no you don't! I believe that is why many people don't ever take the first step. You don't have to redo your photo albums, or get reprints of your photos. The best thing to do is just put all of your photos together and have them handy. Then, you go through the collection, pulling out the ones you need for the video. The most fun way would be to go through the photos with your mom or your grandmother (whoever you're going to feature in your video) letting her select the photos to use. That way you've already got her thinking of her past and the things she might want to talk about.

If she's not available and you need to select the photos yourself, pick out three pictures from when she was a baby and put them in a stack. Get the photos of her parents. Then get a few pictures of her first day of school, first time riding a bike, graduating elementary school, and so on. Add any pictures that the star of the video really likes. Add photos that capture important or funny events that have a story. Look at birthday parties, first pet, weddings, and anything else. Remember, this is a video about your subject for you and future generations to learn the history of the family. Make it fun and interesting! Then, before your first video session, pull out the photos you've selected with her so she knows those are the times in her life you want her to talk about in the video.

Photos are very, very important. Since the video is going to be digital, you want digital copies of your photos. If you don't already have digital copies of the photos you are going to use in the video, you'll want to scan the photos – either yourself or have them done professionally. If your photos have faded or deteriorated over time, you can get them restored or touched up by someone who knows how to use image processing software. If you have digital copies of the photos, most places that print photos will print from digital files for you at a very reasonable cost. Frankly, the only reason to print out digital photos would be to review them with the subject of your video, because you will actually use the digital version in your movie.

If you can't do any of those, see if you can find another photo that is part of the same story or event but is in better condition. Sometimes people store photos from the same event in multiple albums or leave copies in the original photo envelope they received from a photo printing service.

You can sit down with the subject of your video and ask for help putting them in order. Get input on what topics to cover. Maybe your subject really likes caring for children, so you could include photos of the subject with his or her children and grandchildren when they were little. Maybe your subject liked performing music, so you could include photos taken during and after musical performances. Maybe your subject loves cooking, so you could put pictures of your subject cooking a meal for Thanksgiving.

Whatever it is, just be sure that the photos show what your subject is like. If your subject really has a wonderful sense of humor, then have her tell a few funny stories about some of the pictures. Have fun!

Judy Blair

Chapter 8

The Interview

Okay, at this point, you have decided you want a family legacy movie. You have chosen the star of the video, you have chosen your theme, you have set the time, picked a location, and went through the Video Preparation Checklist. And you have all of your photos you'll need for the video. What's next?

Very often, family legacy movies include an interview. An easy way to do the interview is to have one or a few of the subject's children or grandchildren do the interview. Perhaps the video is for Grandma, so her daughter or grandson could sit on a bench with her talking about her life, going through the pictures. You may choose to have the interviewer ask the questions in the background, out of the camera's view. You could place the interviewer on a chair immediately next to the camera so the interviewee will be looking very close to the camera. Their face should be so close so as to be almost touching the camera.

In the interview recording portion, you can bring other things for the subject to talk about. If your subject plays an instrument, maybe she can play a couple of notes. Perhaps you can just record in front of a piano. Objects can make good conversation pieces too. Maybe Grandpa gets his medals out and talks about life during the Korean War.

In fact, I did a legacy video of my husband and his son when he came for a surprise visit. I had the video camera on to record the surprise on my husband's face when he saw his son in our kitchen. That whole day I kept the video camera going. It was just in the corner. No one was really paying attention to it. At one point, his son pulled out his father's old photo album and he started asking him, "Tell me about the Korean War," because he was in the army in the Korean War. As they were going through the pictures my husband was talking about his experiences. I took that video and scanned the photos in to get my digital copies. As he was talking about the picture in the album, that picture is going across the screen so that you can see clearly what was in it.

During the interview, just ask questions. Here are a few sample questions:

- Where were you born?
- Where did you grow up?
- What is your favorite childhood memory?

- Who were your parents? Where did they grow up? Where did they meet?

- When did you get married?

- What are the names of your children?

- What was your first job?

- What was your favorite vacation you have ever taken?

- Were there any struggles or obstacles you had to overcome in your life?

These are just a small sample list of questions. You can get the Video Preparation Checklist at www.KeepsakePix.com/free-pdf.

Here are a few tips on recording.

- If recording indoors, don't record with a window behind the subject's face. This causes the lighting in the video to look bad. It darkens the subject's face and the light from the window makes everything else in the frame look dark. If indoors, sit at a table or on a couch with camera between the window and the subject, with the subject facing the window and camera.

- Check for stray objects. For example, you don't want a full trash can in the background when you're recording in the kitchen. You don't want distracting items lying around on the table or floor in the frame of the camera.

- Wear regular clothes. On video, solid colors and simpler designs work best. If your subject wears makeup, then put on regular makeup. There is nothing wrong with dressing up a little bit for the video, but don't put Grandpa in a tuxedo if he normally just wears jeans and an old t-shirt. Don't have mom put on a ton of clown theater makeup if she normally just puts on a little bit of lipstick. You want the video to look and feel natural. Remember, you're not a lawyer recording a commercial, you're a family member making a video for other family members.

- Make it conversational and relaxed. Enjoy the video! If you have any pauses or go off track, it can always be edited later.

- Record in landscape mode!

- You can record as much or as little as you want. When I work with clients, the final video produced at the end of the process is around an hour long, sometimes divided up into sections. You can record two hours of video or thirty minutes of video. Do what you like. When working with someone to get help with your family legacy movie, the recording can be an hour or two long, maybe longer depending on what you want the video to be like. Don't worry though, it's only one recording session, and that hour of recording will be what you use to keep your legacy available to your future generations!

Chapter 9

How To Construct Your Video

The next step is to put it all together.

After the video is recorded, I normally take the printed photos to be used in the video and scan them to make digital copies. Some people don't feel comfortable handing over their only copies of some of those pictures, so it's a good idea to go somewhere that provides·digital scanning services. The services usually scan with a minimum of 300 dpi (dots per inch.) I've found often that when people scan their own photos either the scanner doesn't have the capability of adjusting the resolution or people just don't know how to adjust it and they give me very poor quality scans, sometimes with 72 dpi. People have given me old 2" x 2" photos scanned at 72 dpi and expect to see a clear photo on their TV. When you put a poor quality photo into a movie and show it on a large TV screen it can be very blurry. So paying attention to scanning quality up front is important.

Once I have digital copies of the photos, the next thing is to match up the video with the pictures. If you go to www.KeepsakePix.com, you can see samples of what videos I've done can look like. It really does bring the pictures to life, and many people just love the end result!

Here's a short story. Betty is a 93 year old woman. She really did not want to have video taken of her because she was embarrassed about her wrinkles. However, her granddaughter did want a legacy video of her grandmother. After months of every now and then raising the subject, her granddaughter said she really wanted to have something to remember her by. She said she would love to have an audiotape even. She agreed to let me videotape her looking at her photo album talking about the photos in her album without videotaping her directly.

That worked out really well. At the end I asked her, "Are you sure you wouldn't like to just do a quick introduction to the family on video? Let me videotape you just saying why you're doing this." She didn't really know what to say so I said, "Why don't you just say something like 'I'm sharing my life in photos for the family'?" I grabbed my smart phone's video camera, captured her saying that, and that was the introduction to the movie. It turns out that this was the only place that she was on video. The rest of it was audio over photos, but it worked out so well that after we showed the video to the family, she realized that she didn't have pictures of her granddaughter in there. She had taken all the pictures of her granddaughter out of her album and put them into an album for the granddaughter. She's done that with her two daughters as well. Finally she agreed to be videotaped for this next video of her sitting with her granddaughter going over their photos. That was progress, and everyone ended up very happy with the end result. It really brings me joy to see families coming together like that.

If you are doing a video on your own, here's what you can do with it after you are done recording:

- Edit the video with basic software that comes with most computers. Add a short introduction clip before the video. There is a bit of a process of learning how to do it, but with some persistence and patience it can be done.

- You can use some royalty-free music that you can find online. Don't use copyrighted music unless you own it and you are going to make a private DVD.

- If you use royalty free music you can then share the video online. YouTube, Vimeo, and other sites will let you upload your video, and you can email links to friends and family or share it on social media.

If putting the movie together still seems daunting, here are some situations where you should consider working with a family legacy movie specialist:

- You have a lot of video recorded, or you have several videos recorded, and you want to make one video out of a lot of material.

- You don't know how to use professional video editing software or you don't want to learn it. Professional videographers have lots of experience with editing software and can render high definition videos for you.

- You want to include extra photos or effects into the video.

- You want to want to insert some special music and don't know how.

A family legacy movie can be a bit of a project, but it's well worth it when it's completed. All of my clients tell me that they, and their families, are so glad they did the legacy movies. For some of them, they did their videos just in time, because the subject of their videos passed weeks or months after the videos were completed. That's why I always say to "do it now!" before it's too late.

Chapter 10

How To Get Help With Your Video

There you have it! A simple guide to getting a family legacy video done.

Sometimes, my clients come to me telling me they started on a video, but just don't know how to finish it.

If you think you might need help, but are not sure if it's a good idea to get help from a video service, here are a few things to consider:

- Are you comfortable with using video editing software?

- Do you know how to scan and touch up digital photos?

- Do you have a high quality camera and microphone? (At the very least a later model iPhone takes quite good quality videos.)

- Do you know how to build an interview scene?

- Can you properly frame a video?

- Do you have a way to properly light the video?

If you don't know what to do or have the proper equipment, the video can come out not quite as good as you initially hoped. There are many people who come up with videos they really like on their own, and that's great! I really hope that this book inspires many people to create their own family legacy movies. It makes me happy to learn that someone has gone and recorded and produced a video for future generations to enjoy.

If you do decide you could use some help, here are some questions to ask before picking a service for help:

- **Do you specialize in family legacy videos?** Most videographers provide a wide range of video services. They'll do corporate training videos, they'll record seminars, some will record physical fitness training videos, some will even work on music videos and some specialize in weddings. That's fine, and many wedding videographers can do an acceptable job with a family legacy movie. But more often than not, I've found that unless someone specializes in family legacy videos, there tends to be something missing. Many videographers rush around in a big hurry to record the video as quickly as possible. Often, family legacy video specialists are more careful with the environment, the preparation for the video, and demonstrate the sensitivity and appreciation for the revelation of personal family information. Recording a family legacy movie can be an emotional and sensitive event, so you really want to work with someone familiar with recording videos in that setting.

- **Am I "just another account," or do you get to know me, my family, and our needs?** There aren't many people providing family legacy movies out there. But for some of them, they have large teams of people who work recording the videos. These can be impersonal encounters, making the legacy video interview seem like a "business transaction" rather than a special moment. I like to learn about my clients, talk with them, hear about their family history, and become a working partner in making their family legacy movie the best it can be. I love working with my clients and we have fun creating the movie. The end result reflects comfort and naturalness because of these factors and everyone feels good about the video project.

- **Who controls the content of my video?** Often, with videographers, there is a strict script for the video being produced. The resulting video can often feel "stiff" and boring. One of the kind things I hear a lot from my clients is that I'm easy to work with. I don't force things on people and we laugh a lot. I work on what the client wants and would never say "Here is what you will do in your video," Rather, I listen to what the client wants and help them decide what would make sense for their video. We work as partners.

- **What if I need guidance?** Many of my clients are local to my area, so I can go in person and help set up the recording scene and shoot the video. But clients also contact me from areas outside of my community, asking for help. I spend time on the phone answering any questions they have, giving suggestions, and sharing tips on improving the video. Out-of-state clients can send me their video recordings and digital image files, then I build the video from there.

What if I have very old family movies?

Here's another story. Meredith's story is one where as a child she said she remembered her grandfather having many reels of old films in a picnic basket. They would look at those films over and over again. Some time ago she had those films converted to VHS tape, and then she brought them to me to convert to DVD.

Then, for her, the magic happened. She looked at the video and I recorded her talking about what was on the video. She was identifying events in old San Jose, old Rose Bowl-type parades that San Jose used to have, and places in San Jose, some of which don't even exist any longer. She was identifying her grandparents and her parents, and her aunts, uncles, and cousins as babies. She was very clear that she wanted to share all those memories with her own children and their kids. She went through this quite extensively. It was a long video. She described everything that was in it. The original movie was a silent movie, so without that description her future generations would not have known what was in that movie other than it was old films. In the end, it was exactly what she wanted, and she was very happy with her movie.

I had another client who was going home for her mother's 90th birthday, but about six months before, she decided in her next visit home she was going to videotape her mother. She had a series of questions that she wanted to ask her mother on video.

She consulted me on what she needed to do and I gave her a list of things to do, like what kind of camera should she get, where should she place it, and so on. Make sure that it's on a tripod or a table or other stable surface. Where should her mother sit? Definitely not in front of a window with glare behind her. That she needed to have her mother against a solid place. It could be a wall. It could be a section of a family room. It doesn't really matter whether there's some background, chairs or other furniture there. The main thing is she would need to arrange to get some light on her mother's face. If she doesn't have professional lighting, she would need to take whatever lights or lamps that she could find in the house and make sure they shined on her mother's face so you could see her face.

That was a combination of long distance and local work because she went to the Midwest, took the video, brought it back to California, and she gave me the files and all the photos. Together, we worked to place all the photos in the correct places in the video. To this day when she talks about it, it brings tears to my eyes because she said when they showed the video at her mother's 90th birthday party, all the children and grandchildren came around and sat near the grandmother and put their arms around her and asked her questions. She says it was the best present she could have given herself. It was very heartwarming.

Chapter 11

The Process

Nothing makes me happier than hearing that someone has successfully created a family legacy movie that will preserve their story and memories for future generations.

Of course there are people who get started, but then get stuck somewhere in the process. Sometimes, clients need someone to finish the video. Sometimes, clients learn that they really don't have the time to create a family legacy movie on their own and then ask me to do it for them.

Here is my process for working with clients.

The first step in the process is my free Legacy Planning Session. This is a session I have with everyone.

It's a free, no-obligations planning session to help you determine how to move forward with your video. If you would like me to create your video for you, or if you just have a few questions and want to get a little bit of guidance so you can make your own, I make these Legacy Planning Sessions available. I dedicate a lot of my time to my existing clients, but I do maintain a few openings every month to offer these free Legacy Planning Sessions. If you are interested in one, just go to www.KeepsakePix.com and request a consultation.

If a client decides they would like me to create the family legacy movie for them, the next step is to meet with the client and the star of the video. We'll talk about what they have in mind for the video, if a family member is going to interview them, either in the movie or behind the scenes, and sometimes we'll look at the photos they've pulled together to talk about in the movie. When I return to shoot the video I might have to rearrange furniture to set the scene for the recording. I ensure that we have a rough outline for the interview, but don't do anything too structured because I want it to be authentic and natural. The family should have already decided on what kinds of questions will be asked so an outline or notes will be helpful for the interviewer.

After the recording session is over, I borrow the original photos or digital copies if they have them. If they are physical photos, I scan them, touching them up so they will look great on screen.

The next step is for me to create the video.

Next we review the first draft of the video. That's

where we ensure that the photos are in the right place. Sometimes we decide we need to add more photos. Some clients have ideas of particular music or songs to be included in the video, or sometimes playing softly in the background of the audio. We can put slides or movie clips in the beginning to introduce the subject, or put slides at the end with other photos.

After the draft phase, I make the changes the client wants. Then after that, we're done! The video is produced! Sometimes the client orders multiple copies of DVDs for other family members.

The process can be as fast or slow as you like. Some of my clients have taken over a year to get everything done just because they needed time to record several sessions, collect pictures from other family members, or any number of reasons. I had one client call me on a Thursday asking to record on a Saturday because his brother would be in town that day and he was supposed to be in the video. Those are extreme examples of course. For many clients, the whole process takes just weeks, depending on how soon we can do the video interview and the draft review.

Judy Blair

Chapter 12

Conclusion

Congratulations, you are well on your way to getting your family legacy movie done! Now, I have a few tips for you.

- Decide you want to do it and take the first step towards accomplishing it.

- Update your photos and old movies by having them digitized.

- Make sure you back up all your photos and all your videos.

- When someone comes to visit or if you have a family reunion, leave the camera running because you don't know what you'll get.

If you'd like to see samples of family legacy videos, go to www.KeepsakePix.com and click the link for "family legacy." If you'd like my Video Preparation Checklist and my Sample Interview Questions Tip Sheet, just go to www.KeepsakePix.com/free. If you'd like to talk to me directly about your family legacy video, go to www.KeepsakePix.com and email me or call me.

One more quick story. I have a client whose mother was not in very good health. She had spoken to her mother and asked her how long she wanted to live. Her mother said, "Until I'm 80." At the time, she was already 79, so when the daughter found out about my service, she called me and asked me to record a video right away. It was only months later that her mother passed away. There is something to be said about doing it as soon as you can. As soon as you know that you want to do it, and especially if you know a loved one is in failing health, do it now. That's my message to you. Do it now, before it's too late.

About The Author

Judy Blair founded KeepsakePix in 2005. She is a mobile videographer located in the Silicon Valley, California. Her passion is creating family legacy movies and creates beautiful keepsake movies for your family and your future generations to share. She believes families need to take action and create their family legacy movies before it is too late.

Judy Blair

To get your free Video Preparation Checklist, go to
www.keepsakepix.com/free.

To get a free consultation about your family legacy movie,
go to www.keepsakepix.com.